I0882797

Strategies to Enhance Air Force Communication with Internal and External Audiences

A WORKSHOP REPORT

Committee on Strategies to Enhance Air Force Communication with Internal and External Audiences: A Workshop

Air Force Studies Board

Division on Engineering and Physical Sciences

The National Academies of
SCIENCES · ENGINEERING · MEDICINE

THE NATIONAL ACADEMIES PRESS
Washington, DC
www.nap.edu

THE NATIONAL ACADEMIES PRESS **500 Fifth Street, NW** **Washington, DC 20001**

This is a report of work supported by Grant FA9550-14-1-0127 between the U.S. Air Force and the National Academy of Sciences. Any opinions, findings, or conclusions expressed in this publication do not necessarily reflect the views of any organization or agency that provided support for the project.

International Standard Book Number-13: 978-0-309-38901-3
International Standard Book Number-10: 0-309-38901-1

Limited copies of this report are available from:

Air Force Studies Board
500 Fifth Street, NW
Washington, DC 20001
(202) 334-3111

Additional copies are available from:

The National Academies Press
500 Fifth Street, NW
Keck 360
Washington, DC 20001
(800) 624-6242 or (202) 334-3313
http://www.nap.edu

Copyright 2016 by the National Academy of Sciences. All rights reserved.

Printed in the United States of America

Suggested citation: National Academies of Sciences, Engineering, and Medicine. 2016. *Strategies to Enhance Air Force Communication with Internal and External Audiences: A Workshop Report.* Washington, DC: The National Academies Press.

The National Academies of
SCIENCES · ENGINEERING · MEDICINE

The **National Academy of Sciences** was established in 1863 by an Act of Congress, signed by President Lincoln, as a private, nongovernmental institution to advise the nation on issues related to science and technology. Members are elected by their peers for outstanding contributions to research. Dr. Ralph J. Cicerone is president.

The **National Academy of Engineering** was established in 1964 under the charter of the National Academy of Sciences to bring the practices of engineering to advising the nation. Members are elected by their peers for extraordinary contributions to engineering. Dr. C. D. Mote, Jr., is president.

The **National Academy of Medicine** (formerly the Institute of Medicine) was established in 1970 under the charter of the National Academy of Sciences to advise the nation on medical and health issues. Members are elected by their peers for distinguished contributions to medicine and health. Dr. Victor J. Dzau is president.

The three Academies work together as the **National Academies of Sciences, Engineering, and Medicine** to provide independent, objective analysis and advice to the nation and conduct other activities to solve complex problems and inform public policy decisions. The Academies also encourage education and research, recognize outstanding contributions to knowledge, and increase public understanding in matters of science, engineering, and medicine.

Learn more about the National Academies of Sciences, Engineering, and Medicine at **www.national-academies.org**.

COMMITTEE ON STRATEGIES TO ENHANCE AIR FORCE COMMUNICATION WITH INTERNAL AND EXTERNAL AUDIENCES: A WORKSHOP

DOUGLAS M. FRASER, U.S. Air Force (retired), *Chair*
PAMELA A. DREW, Premier Aerospace and Defense, *Vice Chair*
RICHARD P. HALLION, Science and Technology Policy Institute
JOANN KEYTON, North Carolina State University
WENDI E. STRONG, USAA

Staff

JOAN FULLER, Director, Air Force Studies Board
ANDREW J. KREEGER, Program Officer
MARGUERITE E. SCHNEIDER, Administrative Coordinator
COURTLAND LEWIS, Consultant
DIONNA C. ALI, Research Assistant

AIR FORCE STUDIES BOARD

DOUGLAS M. FRASER, Doug Fraser, LLC, *Chair*
DONALD C. FRASER, Charles Stark Draper Laboratory (retired), *Vice Chair*
BRIAN A. ARNOLD, Peachtree City, Georgia
ALLISON ASTORINO-COURTOIS, National Security Innovations, Inc.
TED F. BOWLDS, The Spectrum Group
STEVEN R.J. BRUECK, University of New Mexico
FRANK J. CAPPUCCIO, Cappuccio and Associates, LLC
BLAISE J. DURANTE, U.S. Air Force (retired)
BRENDAN B. GODFREY, University of Maryland, College Park
MICHAEL A. HAMEL, Lockheed Martin Space Systems Company
DANIEL E. HASTINGS, Massachusetts Institute of Technology
RAYMOND E. JOHNS, JR., Flight Safety International
ROBERT H. LATIFF, R. Latiff Associates
NANCY G. LEVESON, Massachusetts Institute of Technology
MARK J. LEWIS, Institute for Defense Analyses Science and Technology Policy Institute
ALEX MILLER, University of Tennessee
OZDEN OCHOA, Texas A&M University
RICHARD V. REYNOLDS, The VanFleet Group, LLC
STARNES E. WALKER, University of Delaware
DEBORAH WESTPHAL, Toffler Associates
DAVID A. WHELAN, Boeing Defense, Space, and Security
REBECCA WINSTON, Winston Strategic Management Consulting
MICHAEL I. YARYMOVYCH, Sarasota Space Associates

Staff

JOAN FULLER, Director
ALAN H. SHAW, Deputy Director
DIONNA C. ALI, Research Assistant
GEORGE COYLE, Senior Program Officer
CARTER W. FORD, Program Officer
CHRIS JONES, Financial Manager
ANDREW J. KREEGER, Program Officer
MARGUERITE E. SCHNEIDER, Administrative Coordinator

Acknowledgment of Reviewers

This workshop report has been reviewed in draft form by individuals chosen for their diverse perspectives and technical expertise, in accordance with procedures approved by the Report Review Committee. The purpose of this independent review is to provide candid and critical comments that will assist the institution in making its published report as sound as possible and to ensure that the report meets institutional standards for objectivity, evidence, and responsiveness to the study charge. The review comments and draft manuscript remain confidential to protect the integrity of the deliberative process. We wish to thank the following individuals for their review of this report:

R. Stephen Berry, University of Chicago,
Sharon L. Dunwoody, University of Wisconsin, Madison,
Mark J. Lewis, Science and Technology Policy Institute, and
Rebecca A. Winston, Winston Strategic Management Consulting.

Although the reviewers listed above have provided many constructive comments and suggestions, they were not asked to endorse the views presented at the workshop, nor did they see the final draft of the workshop report before its release. The review of this workshop report was overseen by Chris G. Whipple, ENVIRON (retired), who was responsible for making certain that an independent examination of this workshop report was carried out in accordance with institutional procedures and that all review comments were carefully considered. Responsibility for the final content of this report rests entirely with the committee and the institution.

Contents

APPENDIXES

Acronyms

AFRC	Air Force Recruiting Command
CSAF	Chief of Staff of the Air Force
NCO	non commissioned officer
PA	Public Affairs
SCARF	status, certainty, autonomy, relatedness, and fairness
USAF	United States Air Force

Overview

The U.S. Air Force (USAF) helps defend the United States and its interests by organizing, training, and equipping forces for operations in and through three distinct domains—air, space, and cyberspace. The Air Force concisely expresses its vision as "Global Vigilance, Global Reach, and Global Power for America." This vision is divided by the distinct capabilities, knowledge, equipment, and training needed to operate in each of the three domains. The specialization within these areas affects most Airmen's understanding of the overall Air Force mission and its complexity, as well as their roles in the Service. Operations within each domain are dynamic, take place over large distances, occur over different operational timelines, and cannot be routinely seen or recorded, making it difficult for Airmen, national decision makers, and the American people to visualize and comprehend the full scope of Air Force operations. As a result, the Air Force faces increasing difficulty in succinctly and effectively communicating the complexity, dynamic range, and strategic importance of its mission to Airmen and to the American people.

To address this concern, the Chief of Staff of the U.S. Air Force (CSAF) requested that the National Academies of Sciences, Engineering, and Medicine convene a workshop to explore options on how the Air Force can effectively communicate the strategic importance of the Service, its mission, and the role it plays in the defense of the United States. The answer to this question is complex, difficult to state simply, and difficult to describe for each of the operational domains, much less how the Air Force integrates operations across domains. This workshop was developed to address the issue that a diverse workforce encompassing a myriad of backgrounds, education, and increasingly diverse current mission sets drives the requirement for a new communication strategy. In fact, the demographics of today's Air Force creates both a unique opportunity and a distinct challenge to Air Force leadership as it struggles to communicate its vision and strategy effectively across several micro-cultures within the organization and to the general public. The role of communication in describing the Air Force mission to both internal and external stakeholders has not been well addressed within the military community.

The Committee on Strategies to Enhance Air Force Communication with Internal and External Audiences, composed of experts in organizational behavior, military doctrine, communication, public relations, and other relevant areas, was appointed by the Academies in July 2015 under the auspices of the Air Force Studies Board. The committee planned and participated in the workshop and prepared this report. The workshop was held on September 2-4, 2015, in Washington, D.C. Approximately 40 participants, including speakers, committee members, invited guests, and members of the public, attended the 3-day workshop. Workshop speakers were asked by the committee to give presentations that would respond to one or more of the following questions:

1. Why is communicating across the generations important to the Air Force's future? What is the strategic imperative to do so?
2. What makes communicating in today's Air Force different now as compared to other periods in history?
3. What proven strategies exist for effectively communicating a complex set of issues to both internal and external audiences? Identify tools and activities that are most appropriate for the Air Force to communicate key messages to its various audiences.
4. Are there examples of other organizations that are addressing this challenge? Identify options for potential actions the Air Force can take based on these best practices by others.
5. What is the role of social media[1] in implementing an effective communication strategy? What role can social media play within the context of developing an effective communication strategy for a military organization?
6. What should be the Air Force's measures of success in its strategic communication plan? How should the Air Force measure effectiveness with both internal and external audiences?

The scope of the workshop focused on policies, practices, and technologies that could be applicable to communication in the Air Force. Consequently, representatives of the USAF Public Affairs (PA) office were invited to present on the current status of and plans for this office and the Air Force generally.

The workshop report begins with a discussion of the importance of an Air Force-wide communication strategy, the current status quo, and the challenges the Air Force will face in developing and implementing such a strategy, should it choose to do so. Chapter 2 describes the issues involved in communicating the value and essence of the Air Force to a wide diversity of audiences, both internally and externally, including the lessons learned by various large corporations with similar communication goals. Chapter 3 outlines possible organizational strategies and processes for implementing a communication strategy in the Air Force, with a special focus on social media. Chapter 4 outlines available tools and techniques for measuring the effectiveness of communication in and by large organizations such as the Air Force.

This report summarizes the views expressed by individual workshop participants. While the committee is responsible for the overall quality and accuracy of the report as a record of what transpired at the workshop, the views contained in the report are not necessarily those of all workshop participants, the committee, or the Academies.

[1] *Social media*, as defined by Merriam-Webster, are forms of electronic communication through which users create online communities to share information, ideas, personal messages, and other content.

1

Challenges in Developing and Evaluating an Effective Communication Strategy for the U.S. Air Force

This workshop was initiated at the request of the Chief of Staff of the U.S. Air Force (CSAF) Gen. Mark Welsh and prompted by several ongoing concerns he has regarding communication across the Air Force. Gen. Welsh expressed those concerns in person to the workshop participants. In summary, they are as follows:

- The CSAF has found difficulty in getting information from his level to wing commanders and, in turn, to other supervisors and Airmen in general.[1] As a result, too few senior leaders and supervisors receive the information from the CSAF and Air Staff.
- The CSAF has also found difficulty in communicating to the American people the value of the Air Force and the complexity of the mission that the Air Force accomplishes on a routine basis.
- Finally, the CSAF is concerned about inaccurate, incomplete, or misleading outside information published about the Air Force that is often read and believed by Airmen.

During the course of the 3-day workshop, common messages, or themes, appeared as a result of various presentations and resulting dialogue among the participants. Each theme represents an integrated summary of the presentations and discussion. They should not be construed as reflecting consensus or endorsement by the committee, the workshop participants, or the National Academies of Sciences, Engineering, and Medicine. Supporting details precede each theme in the report.

U.S. AIR FORCE COMMUNICATION PRACTICES: CURRENT STATUS

Gen. Welsh recognizes that four key characteristics of communication within a large organization are clarity, reach, speed, and impact—with the latter being perhaps the most important but also the most difficult to measure. He noted that effective communication must link words with actions. At the same time, it must be as clear and transparent as policy and security will allow.

Official U.S. Air Force (USAF) communication channels today, he said, include base newsletters, weekly guidance issued by the Public Affairs (PA) office, press releases, and the AF.mil website. The USAF relies heavily

[1] Because of the breadth of topics discussed and time limitations of the workshop, the specific information and expectations of who is responsible for receiving and understanding this information was not discussed.

on email for official internal communication. The USAF PA office is headquartered at the Pentagon and led by Brig. Gen. Kathleen Cook, who gave a presentation and attended all but the last two presentations of the workshop. The primary responsibility of the PA office is communicating the Air Force message to the public, in particular through the news media. Communication for recruiting purposes (e.g., advertising) is the responsibility of the Air Force Recruiting Command (AFRC).

Air Force communication is both internal—to and from members of the Air Force, both operationally and for imparting general information—and external, from the Air Force to Congress, potential recruits, and the public at large. As Workshop Vice Chair Dr. Pamela Drew noted, "The purpose of external communication is *inspiration*; the focus of internal communication is *execution*." Gen. Welsh made it clear that his primary concerns relate to internal communication, with external communication being of secondary interest.

It became clear through discussion with Gen. Welsh and Gen. Cook that there is at present no overall USAF communication strategy "connecting the dots" of internal and external communication with the decisions and actions of the Air Force. Internal communication is siloed within the many operational commands spread across the Air Force's different operating domains and around the world.

Externally, as described by Gen. Cook and other participants, the Air Force uses several slogans or vision statements for different purposes, including "Aim High . . . Fly, Fight, Win"; "Global Vigilance, Global Reach, and Global Power for America"; "World's Greatest Air Force: Powered by Airmen, Fueled by Innovation"; and the simplest, "One Air Force" and "Above All." However, there is not a single core message that describes succinctly the essence of the Air Force and that permeates and connects its communications. Nor has senior leadership established a consistent set of priorities for communication.

A common discussion point among several Air Force participants as well as non-Air Force participants was the current level of authority afforded to the PA office. Most fundamentally, there is no locus at the highest levels of the Air Force, as committee member Ms. Wendi Strong explained, for the alignment of strategic communication priorities between the CSAF and the Secretary of the Air Force, for agreement on strategic goals, and for the debate and adoption of an overall communication strategy supporting a broad "Air Force narrative." Figure 1-1 illustrates that lack of alignment. Gen. Welsh recognized this shortcoming and welcomed advice from the workshop participants.

U.S. AIR FORCE COMMUNICATION CHALLENGES: TODAY AND FUTURE

Gen. Welsh reiterated the challenges with both internal and external communication. "Internally," he said, "getting information to the wing commanders is a big frustration." To move toward what he termed "active communication," Gen. Welsh discussed a recently developed web-based tool on which information is posted and an email message is generated to all commanders that the message is there. He expects them to read and acknowledge receipt of the information. "I think it's essential to keep our Airmen fully informed of decisions we make relating to the budget and the impacts it will have on them. Our people are really smart, they like information, and they're used to getting it quickly." However, as noted by a workshop participant, the conventional internal media are not meeting that need. For example, Gen. Welsh related, only about 10 percent of the attendees at an Air Force-wide Wing Commanders Conference said they have ever read the PA guidance that is sent out weekly by email. The *Air Force Times*, an independent news and information source, is widely read, but it is not an official USAF product and can disseminate inaccurate information that is discussed and believed, Gen. Welsh said.

Capt. Samuel "Ross" Hubbard, speaking on behalf of the younger corps of officers and non-commissioned officers (NCOs), said, "We understand the Air Force mission and vision. What we don't understand is how to take the objectives of senior leadership and square those with the mission and vision, and then with our own jobs." He said that when he asks his leadership for that kind of information, "they don't have it; we're not receiving the message that Gen. Welsh thinks we're receiving." The Air Force communicates mainly by email, but "to convert you to the mission, I have to meet you face to face. You have to convert me before I can convert my friends."

Social media present a different level of concern that is related to this communication disconnect. These platforms—Twitter, Snapchat, Facebook, blogs—are barely used at all by the official Air Force today; yet the Air Force workforce uses them ubiquitously. They are used not only for purely social interaction of a personal nature, but

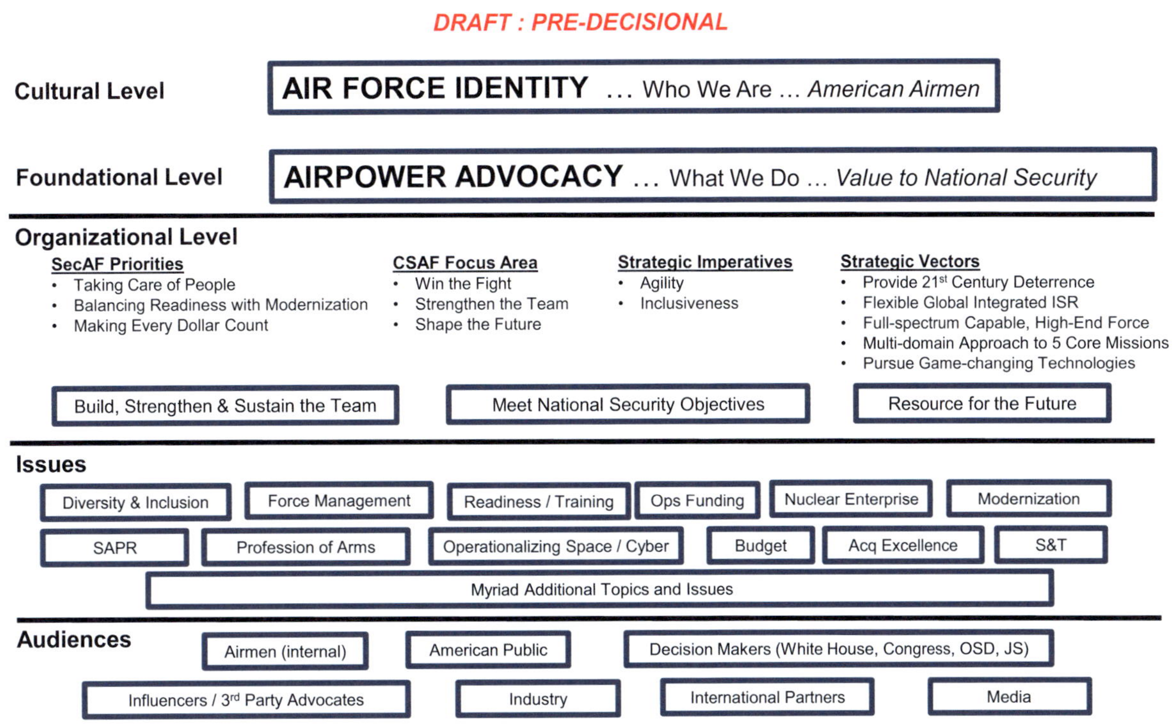

FIGURE 1-1 Graphical depiction of the Air Force communication landscape. SOURCE: Brig. Gen. Kathleen Cook, Air Force Public Affairs. Used with permission.

also to complain about aspects of their jobs. Gen. Welsh referred to Airmen "slamming each other and their bosses on blogs like Yik Yak." He said the reach of these tools is so great that such communications quickly spread false information that is readily believed and further disseminated by others, ultimately reaching parents, the media, and lawmakers. Gen. Cook described the many difficulties that responding to this misinformation creates for her office.

Regarding external communication, Gen. Welsh said, "The problem is how to explain a very complex mission set to a very different set of audiences." Many participants stated that the main problem is the lack of one simple and compelling message—a brand—to describe the Air Force. As committee member Dr. Richard Hallion noted, "The other services have an overarching, unifying identity. The other services also give a human face to their public image." The Air Force tends to stress innovation and technology, not people. These images do not convey the essence of the Air Force or provide a compelling reason for audiences to care about the organization and its people, Dr. Hallion said.

Finally, Gen. Welsh asked the workshop to consider the question, "How do we know when we're doing it [communicating] right?" He concluded by saying, "I don't feel like we're an adaptive organization when it comes to communication."

KEY CHALLENGES DISCUSSED: CULTURE, ORGANIZATION, AND STRATEGY

Ensuing discussion on key challenges involved the committee members and other participants with Gen. Welsh and presenters Brig. Gen. Cook, Lt. Gen. Steven Kwast, Maj. Gen. Mari Eder (U.S. Army, retired), Dr. Vernon Miller, Dr. Alan Vick, former Air Force Secretaries James Roche and F. Whitten Peters, Col. Sean Monogue, and Capt. Hubbard.

Beginning with internal communication, Gen. Kwast said that the Air Force's internal communication problem "is an organizational and cultural problem. It is not a public affairs problem." Workshop Chair Gen. Douglas

Fraser (USAF, retired) noted the Air Force's problem goes beyond the current scope of public affairs and added, "Too much of internal communication has been delegated to Public Affairs vice commanders and supervisors." Gen. Welsh agreed that there are serious gaps in communication and that mechanisms are needed "to get the right information to the right people at the right time." Ms. Strong added that holding leadership accountable for communication is clearly important; the question is how to do it. Additionally, Dr. Hallion commented that young Airmen see only their own roles but do not know where they fit into the overall picture. As Gen. Fraser stated, "The rank and file Airmen understand the Air Force mission and message. They don't understand how senior-level decisions support or improve their ability to do the mission. They don't know where to go online or offline to get the official Air Force position."

Workshop participant Ms. Deborah Westphal, chief executive officer of Toffler Associates, asked what Gen. Welsh would like to see in this area in 5 years. He replied, "Airmen [should] feel comfortable knowing where information on big issues, big problems can be found." A significant part of the solution would be that commanders and supervisors have to "proactively communicate—it's part of your job description." The workforce, by and large, does not go to AF.mil, where policy- and budget-related information resides. For example, Col. Monogue, chief for strategy and assessments for Air Force Public Affairs, noted that on AF.mil there is a smart-phone app called AFLink, which has been downloaded only 5,000 times. Consequently, Col. Monogue added, "Supervisors need to have the mindset that they have a responsibility to get this information to their people."

A key issue identified by some participants is the ability of the Air Force workforce to trust what their leadership tells them, and to have confidence that they can ask questions and express opinions without repercussions. As Ms. Strong suggested, "Trust should be cultivated through communications that are *authentic* and *transparent*. That means telling people what you know, when you know it, in human terms and voice, with context and a focus on the "Why?" That trustworthiness, Ms. Westphal noted, requires a willingness to admit mistakes and a lack of complete knowledge—something that senior leaders in any organization are usually reluctant to do. Several workshop participants added that transparency, as described by Ms. Strong, may not always be achievable within a government organization.

Regarding external communication, former Secretary James Roche noted, "There's no such thing as internal communication that's separate from external communication. The one drives the other." Gen. Fraser made the point that we arm Air Force personnel with powerful, expensive weapons, train them to use them, and hold them accountable, "but we're not willing to do the same with communication and information."

Using as an example the issue of budget cuts to programs, which are a frequent source of complaints from the workforce on social media, former Secretary Peters said, "From the top down, the program trade-offs make sense; but from the bottom up, they don't. This leads to a two-fold problem: (1) How do we explain what we do, and why we're doing it, to Congress, the press, and other stakeholders? and (2) How do we explain it to the troops so that they understand?" The issue of trust also applies to communication with the public.

The discussion of disconnects in communication upward and downward, internally and externally, led the committee to take a broader look at what underlies these problems. Many participants expressed the view that what the Air Force lacks is a "culture of communication," one driven from the top leadership by an overarching communication strategy, anchored with a clear, compelling brand, that ties all elements of Air Force communication together in an integrated way. As Ms. Strong stated, "There may be a number of organizational goals that communications can help achieve, but there must be clear objectives with defined outcomes. And those objectives must be agreed upon by the most senior level leadership of the Air Force." Leaders should take ownership of and responsibility for communication as an integral part of Air Force operations and should ensure that communication objectives are met. A strong culture of communication also engenders loyalty on the part of the workforce, reducing the spread of the negative and inaccurate information that concerns Gen. Welsh and other Air Force leaders.

Theme 1—Culture of Communication. Many participants expressed the view that the USAF lacks a culture of communication—a culture in which every leader or supervisor is responsible and accountable for communicating within the organization. Based on several participants' statements, senior leaders do not "own" communication as an essential part of Air Force operations—that is, they do not integrate it into the overall Air Force strategy. Consequently, there is no real commitment to messaging internally or externally in a consistent and deliberate way. Infusing a culture of communication throughout the Air Force would mean that communication is free flowing within the organization and understood as everyone's responsibility, for which leaders are accountable. Such a culture is built on a foundation of trust at the Airman level. Trust, in turn, is best cultivated through communications that are authentic and transparent, conveyed with a human and personal voice, with a realistic context and a focus on the "Why?" Ultimately, actions matter more than words, and the two have to be closely aligned and integrated in order to maintain the trust of highly "connected" and aware Airmen. Trust is a two-way street; in such a culture, every participant feels a responsibility to protect the reputation of the organization.

During discussions on the current organizational structure and responsibilities within the Air Force, several participants noted that the Air Force does not currently have a single-point coordinating group that works with senior Air Force leaders to set communication policies and plans and oversee their execution. Additionally, these participants remarked that communications leadership does not currently have a seat at the most senior-level tables and does not hold senior-level positions commensurate with other core, essential functions. They emphasized the importance of an organization having adequate resources for planning, execution, and measurement.

Workshop participant Ms. Rebecca Winston, president of Winston Strategic Management Consultants, pointed out that communication in the Air Force differs from that of other operations—it is not handled as a program. Instead, it is a diffuse enterprise that cuts across all operations and is not integrated across the enterprise for all audiences. Ms. Strong added that the PA function does not have accountability for all messaging to all audiences through all channels. There is no organization-wide communications function, resulting in weakly structured and coordinated internal communications. The communications organization is under-resourced and needs to be modernized in terms of organizational structure, processes, and tools, Ms. Strong said. It is evident, she concluded, that the Air Force does not value communication very highly.

Theme 2—Organizational Responsibility. Several participants noted that Air Force communication leadership currently does not have frequent or reliable access to senior leaders and executive-level meetings or hold senior positions commensurate with other core functions of the Air Force such as personnel or operations. As highlighted by some presenters, given the lack of integration and access, the USAF PA office is often assigned responsibility for tasks that it does not have the authority or sufficient resources to execute efficiently, while other important functions are unassigned and not performed. These participants also highlighted the importance of having adequate resources for planning, execution, and measurement within an organization.

An important aspect of the discussions centering on the key challenges facing the Air Force was the need for a communication strategy. As previously discussed, the Air Force does not currently have a point for the alignment of strategic communication priorities among the senior-most leadership. The following question was raised by the committee: "Is there a difference between a crisis strategy and an enduring strategy?" Dr. Brian Hoey, principal of the Hoey Group, believes that an organization can map a long-term strategy but must be willing and able to adapt it—to build in flexibility for contingencies. "The crisis is always about to hit—you just don't know it," he said. Dr. Pamela Drew noted that in a crisis, transparency and authenticity are crucial.

Theme 3—Communication Strategy. As discussed between the participants from the USAF and several participants from industry, the USAF does not have a coherent communication strategy encompassing both internal and external communication and the diverse audiences it must engage. As a result, there is not one, clear set of organizational objectives owned by the senior-most leadership. Responsibility for external communication is divided between the PA office (for media) and the AFRC (for recruiting). Internal communication is stovepiped at the operational command level, where it is ad hoc, subject specific, and disconnected from the Airmen workforce. Several other participants noted that, in general, a communication strategy should improve the performance of an organization and contain outcome-oriented goals tailored to specific audiences. Additionally, they noted that an effective communication strategy is centrally owned and governed with decentralized execution—focused on desired outcomes and impact, not just education and information.

2

Communicating with a Wide Spectrum of Audiences

A fundamental question is, "Why does communication matter?" As Dr. Alan Vick, senior political scientist at the RAND Corporation, explained, every government agency has a responsibility to go to the nation and explain why the taxpayers *need* to support that agency. In addition, leaders have more effective communication with their subordinates when they can start with an explanation of why what they do is important.

There are multiple audiences for the U.S. Air Force (USAF) message, both internally (commanders, supervisors, and Airmen) and externally (friends and family, the media, lawmakers, potential recruits, retirees, allies, and the public in general). This chapter of the workshop report will address some of the issues related to communicating with those diverse audiences.

ISSUES IN DESCRIBING THE VALUE OF THE U.S. AIR FORCE MISSION TO DIVERSE AUDIENCES

Today's frenetic communications environment makes it more difficult than ever for an organization to break through with its messages. Many of the industry experts participating in the workshop stated that communications—not only external ones, but also internal ones—must be compelling, highly relevant, personalized, and action-oriented. This points to the issue of branding, introduced in the previous chapter. The experts noted that communicating the complexity of the Air Force to multiple audiences and inspiring their support is no easy task; it requires a unifying theme. Dr. Brian Hoey noted that the more complex the organization and its mission, the greater the importance of projecting a clear, compelling message. The emotional content of the brand—what presenter Mr. William Power, senior partner at Fleishman-Hillard, called "communicating the core values of an organization"—is becoming more important than the literal and practical meaning of the brand. As Gen. Douglas Fraser noted, "There is a lot of art in communicating." Mr. Peter Debreceny, senior partner at Gagen-MacDonald, said, "The Air Force narrative has to be coherent mentally but also inspiring emotionally."

Many workshop participants stated that development of a simple, compelling brand for the Air Force that can speak to all generations should be a priority. A variety of messages could then be developed and tailored to different audiences, but still be tied to this overarching theme. Mr. William Power and Ms. Wendi Strong discussed the importance of being able to make a clear connection between the specifically tailored messages and the overarching brand, with clearly defined and measurable expected outcomes for each message—and then making those measurements and tying the results back to the evolution of the messaging. Strategies could be developed that communicate value to specific audiences in ways that drive desired outcomes beyond a basic level of understanding.

Mr. Power compared the advertising/recruiting "pitches" of the Marines, Army, and Air Force. The first two, he said, appeal to the viewer directly, in a human way. As an example, Mr. Power used the Air Force's past theme "Above All" and noted that it is more amorphous; the objective of the message is unclear. It sounds "corporate," he said, as though the target audience is Congress and the objective is the budget. He noted that the high-tech image of the Air Force is both positive and negative in this sense; there needs to be a balance. Ms. Strong suggested, "Public Affairs should challenge the idea you have to choose between the excitement of high-tech and the trust and loyalty that a more human-centered approach engenders."

Ms. Rebecca Winston focused strongly on the importance of storytelling. "What we're missing is the compelling stories that the public can relate to." Young audiences in particular, she said, need heroes and role models with a human face. James Roche, former Secretary of the USAF, suggested telling the Air Force story "as if you were raising money for a company project: 'This is something you want to invest in, and here's why.'"

He elaborated further that one might view the Air Force as a portfolio of businesses, from space to special tactics, with Air Combat, Air Mobility, and the battlefield Airman in between; this could be an effective way to approach the issue of mission diversity in developing an Air Force brand.

The fact that top Air Force leadership rotates also emphasizes the importance of having a codified, strong brand that leaders at all levels buy into emotionally and intellectually, with the understanding that it will be central to the organization long into the future. Gen. Fraser noted that this means that an entire cadre of top leadership has to accept that core brand.

> **Theme 4—Brand.** Several participants compared the USAF with the other military services and noted that the USAF does not have a single, clear, and compelling unifying theme or message—a brand—especially one that is closely aligned both internally and externally. This is partly a function of the diverse domains and complex multiple missions of the Air Force, and partly a function of its high-tech nature. As several other participants noted, a brand need not encompass every aspect of the Air Force's mission,[1] but it should be able to reflect the essence of the Air Force in a way that "Aim High . . . Fly, Fight, Win" does not. Additionally, they noted, messages can be tailored to different audiences and tied back to the single unifying theme, or brand, in order to inspire, inform, and remain emotionally relevant.

INTERNAL COMMUNICATION: U.S. AIR FORCE STAKEHOLDERS

All of the communication experts who participated at the workshop voiced the opinion that everyone in an organization, including leadership at every level, has a role in effective communication. They said that "people leaders" are essential. Often in organizations, the most important and effective person in the communication chain (ideally, the chain of command) whom employees look to for information and leadership is their immediate supervisor. It was discussed among participants that immediate supervisors should help Airmen "connect the dots" between their day-to-day work and the greater Air Force mission. These supervisors form the intermediate level between policy makers and the doers who carry out the mission, but often they do not have the needed information or are reluctant to communicate it. Mr. Brian Ames, vice president of employee communications for the Boeing Company, said that Boeing managers are told that communication is not an additional task; "It's what you do."

Mr. Debreceny stated that internal communication in an organization used to be the least important part of communication. Now it is the most important part, the "critical enabler" linking an organization's strategy, culture, and structure. "Organizations must provide clarity, information, and inspiration," he said, so that employees can answer three questions: "What do I need to know?" "What do I need to do?" and "Why should I care?" Mr. Ryan Henary, managing director of internal communications for FedEx Ground, revealed that 20 people in his organization are now responsible for internal communication, while only 6 handle external communication—a reversal from just a few years ago. Brig. Gen. Kathleen Cook reiterated that no one in the Air Force "owns" inter-

[1] An assessment of historical USAF public narratives was presented by Dr. Alan Vick. Details of this assessment may be found in the 2015 RAND Corporation report *Proclaiming Airpower: Air Force Narratives and American Public Opinion from 1917 to 2014,* written by Dr. Vick.

nal communication. A few of the other workshop participants stated that the owner of the strategy should be the senior Air Force leadership.

Mr. Debreceny said that informal messaging is much more powerful today than formal messaging. Again, he said that leadership must be authentic: "If you say, 'We're going to be different than we were,' then you have to *be* different." Further, if organizations are to be transparent, then they must expose "the good, the bad, and the ugly." Otherwise, he said there is no credibility. Mr. Debreceny concluded by noting that in order to gain that credibility and the trust that comes with it, actions matter far more than words; the two must be aligned.

Again, many participants stated that stories are an important vehicle. Maj. Gen. Mari Eder, former head of communications for the U.S. Army, said that stories that go "up" from Airmen are as important as those produced by the PA office; there needs to be a conduit and the means to use them.

Many participants highlighted the importance of maintaining face-to-face interactions and communications between supervisors and Airmen on a routine basis. Face-to-face communication results in buy-in, while email is seen as transactional. They noted that this type of in-person communication is more effective in helping Airmen gain trust and confidence in the information they receive. Several participants added that, although they should not replace face-to-face interactions, social media offer a rich array of options for reaching people of all ages both internally and externally. In addition, because exchanges on social media are highly trackable, trends in attitudes as well as influential people can be identified and incorporated into the communication strategy. Gen. Cook said that Air Force policy for social media exists, but it is unclear, resulting in the underutilization of these media.

In today's world it is not enough to "push" out strategic communication. The internal audience will circulate and discuss it and will often interpret it inaccurately. The way to deal with that, Mr. Debreceny suggested, is to keep the communication going and to link the internal audience into the strategy to heighten understanding. Employees want to know "What's in it for me?" You, as the communicator, want to know "What do we want *them* to know, to do, and to feel?"

Ms. Rebecca Winston said that the reason for emphasizing internal communication more is that what other people say within the organization is what the workforce believes is the accepted truth, and they will act on that. Therefore, she said, it is crucial to get ahead of the uninformed discussion. She noted that you cannot control individual biases, but in general you can influence the environment (and thus the culture).

Dr. Hoey emphasized the value of identifying key "influencers" in the workplace to help develop strategy for both internal and external communication. Often such people are not in the chain of command. Engage them, place confidence in them, and make them part of the communication team, he advised. They are often sensitive to the unintended consequences of policy decisions and can help leadership understand the personal concerns and fears of the workplace that lead to negative communications.

Theme 5—Internal Communication. As noted by Mr. Debreceny, internal communications in large organizations have become more important than official external communications, but several other workshop participants voiced the view that the USAF has not adequately addressed this shift in emphasis. Airmen by and large understand what the Air Force is and does. But they are narrowly focused on their job, communicate most often with their immediate cohorts, and often do not understand the connection between their work and the larger purpose and mission of the Air Force. Their connection to Air Force policy and purpose is primarily face-to-face, through their supervisor—and this continues to be the most trusted and effective form of communication. But, as discussed by some of the participants, supervisors often do not realize the implications of policies on their unit's work and consequently do not communicate that clearly to the workforce. As a result, Airmen's communications among themselves and with their networks via social media are unmanaged and sometimes appear to be unjustifiably negative. Communications "up" as well as outward from the workforce to the public are increasingly important compared to traditional communication down through the chain of command. As discussed by Dr. Hoey, involving internal "influencers" outside the chain of command in the communication process is one method that companies have used to facilitate stronger internal messaging.

EXTERNAL COMMUNICATION

In this context it is necessary to remember the distinction between formal external communication, with which the PA office and the Air Force Recruiting Command (AFRC) are charged, and the informal external communication conducted largely by Airmen, primarily through social media. Although internal and external communications now drive each other and overlap to a considerable extent, as former Secretary Roche noted earlier, these two channels will never coincide; however, said committee member Dr. Joann Keyton, ideally they should be aligned. That said, she continued, it is important to ask, "What communication skills do Airmen need for different communication tasks at different levels?"

Several participants discussed the importance of storytelling and how to go about it. Ms. Winston stressed that presenting real-world examples of Air Force personnel overcoming great odds to achieve their missions would be an effective way to carry the message. Use real people as the storytellers, Mr. Debreceny urged. As Mr. Power stated, use as few words as possible; think of stories as "vignettes."

The image, or brand, issue is pertinent here. Capt. Hubbard said that, in his view, branding is only important for external audiences: "The people inside already know what the Air Force is. We don't need slogans; we need information about *why* we do what we do. If you convert us (the Airmen), we can help you with the external communications task."

Face-to-face communication is very powerful for external audiences as well as internal audiences. Capt. Samuel "Ross" Hubbard noted that there is fear on the part of junior officers and enlisted personnel about telling the Air Force story, because so much information is restricted. In addition, Gen. Cook added, if senior officers display a reluctance to speak externally on an official basis, then that reluctance will tend to be transmitted to their subordinates.

> **Theme 6—External Communication.** Several participants noted that increasingly, as was shown through examples in other organizations, internal and external communications overlap and merge. Because of the pervasive use of social media, there are no longer boundaries between the two. These participants also noted that airmen are potentially the best and most direct channel for positive communication with external as well as internal audiences, and the best advocates for the Air Force with the public. As noted earlier while discussing issues in describing the value of the USAF, several participants expressed the view that a powerful way to tell the Air Force story, both internally and externally, is through the use of "storytelling" involving Air Force people doing interesting or even extraordinary, "heroic" things. Graphics are becoming more effective than words, and words should be minimized to reduce messages to their essence.

ROLE OF SOCIAL MEDIA IN COMMUNICATION TODAY

Several speakers noted the importance of recognizing generational differences for preferred methods of communicating information. As previously discussed, Capt. Hubbard noted that the majority of information in the Air Force is communicated via email, but that is not necessarily the preferred method to convey information to younger Airmen. Several participants highlighted the need to address the differences among generations and how the use of social media is often more prolific among younger Airmen, both for internal and external communication.

Related to this issue, several workshop participants, to include leaders of social media development and management in industry, described to the committee how some organizations are exploring and using innovative ways to communicate with both internal and external audiences and how others are just beginning to explore the potential. Mr. Robert Harles, global head of social media for Accenture Digital, said that the key to social media is that "people want to know they matter." Social media is now at an inflection point, he said, in which it is moving from a "grassroots" use to a more traditional function in companies. Ms. Lois Kelly, chief executive officer of Foghound, said that whereas different modes of communication in companies used to be separate divisions (print advertising, employee communication, public affairs, etc.), now they are merging. Social media are helping to drive that shift. They offer new options for how to deliver the message, which is what gives the message impact and has consequently changed the communication landscape. She added that social media are highly valued as tools for building internal and external networks and for collaborative problem-solving. Advances in measurement and analysis options for communications have facilitated this mainstreaming of social media in business.

As Mr. Ed Terpening, industry analyst for the Altimeter Group, noted, "Social media is a relationship-building tool more than a communication tool." He described three types of relationships that are central to the use of social media—internal collaboration, external engagement, and a third new area, employee advocacy (social recruiting, referrals, etc.). Mr. Terpening said that the governance structure of organizations often is not ready for and therefore resists the introduction of social media. Introducing social media requires "new skills at every level." To provide such education for the leadership, he recommends using "reverse mentors" (i.e., young employees who can help executives understand the range of platforms and uses of social media), rather than workshops.

Mr. Ed Brill, vice president of social business cloud services at IBM, defined a social business as "an organization whose culture of participation and systems of engagement encourage networks of people to create business outcomes." He said that to determine the return on investment for implanting social media, it is necessary to have real outcomes. Mr. Brill said that IBM's social media platforms have become the baseline communication mechanism for the entire company.

Ms. Kelly observed that, usually, we acquire a new technology and then try to figure out what problem to solve with it. Social media are no different; we have to think about "What are the strategic objectives, and how can these tools support those objectives?" Ms. Kelly described two social media best practices as (1) measuring what matters in communication and (2) sharing good stories. Nowadays, she noted, some of the brightest people in companies—people whom management can trust—are put in charge of social media.

A big challenge in organizational use of social media for communication, Mr. Harles said, is reputation management. Changes in the public (and employee) view of the organization can happen instantly. Social media can both cause and manage this. He stated that two other important challenges are (1) insuring that you have sufficient resources and (2) laying the groundwork for the future.

Theme 7—General Role of Social Media. The social media experts participating in the workshop stated that social media are no longer separate and distinct from mainstream communication; they have become an integral part of the communication ecosystem and are a main component of communication at all levels today, for business as well as for personal use, to build networks and to strengthen collaborative problem-solving. In many large companies, social media are no longer seen as peripheral or optional, but as core functions. Social analytic tools and technologies have developed to a degree of sophistication such that they can now be used to gain real-time insight into communication effectiveness.

3

Organizational Strategies and Processes for Enhancing U.S. Air Force Communication Effectiveness

The foregoing chapters of this report have outlined the rationale for developing a communication strategy for the U.S. Air Force (USAF) and the challenges in doing so, given the wide diversity of the missions and audiences that the Air Force must address. This chapter will explore specific elements of a possible strategy for increasing the effectiveness of USAF communication, with a particular focus on social media. Lessons learned by other large organizations that have faced comparable issues will be presented.

LESSONS LEARNED BY OTHER ORGANIZATIONS

Several professional communicators from major corporations and communication consulting firms briefed the workshop participants on best practices used by their organizations and lessons they have learned through their experiences. These presentations and discussions are summarized in this section, with each lesson learned followed by the discussion around that topic.

Responsibility of Communication Within an Organization

As presented by several participants, communication is everyone's responsibility in an organization, and that responsibility begins with leadership. Mr. Brian Ames said that Boeing's strategies "drive a value chain seeking to connect communications with organizational performance." They outline specific communications roles for executives, managers, and the workforce. In addition, Boeing's "strategic measurement" of communication is tied to its semi-annual engagement metrics, which are used, in part, to determine management rewards, he said.

Dr. Brian Hoey gave several examples of good organizational communication practices. For example, when NASA has a public relations issue, it puts scientific, management, and public affairs people together in a room and identifies the best spokespeople on that issue.

In talking about what the C-suite (senior leadership) wants from the communications function today, Mr. Peter Debreceny of Gagen-MacDonald noted that many communication leaders are not sufficiently versed in the business aspects of what makes the organization succeed. Mr. Debreceny described the typical taxonomy of a corporate communications and public affairs department today, a unit that is responsible for executing all communication and is typically at the level of all other key corporate functions such as marketing and sales or human resources (see Figure 3-1).

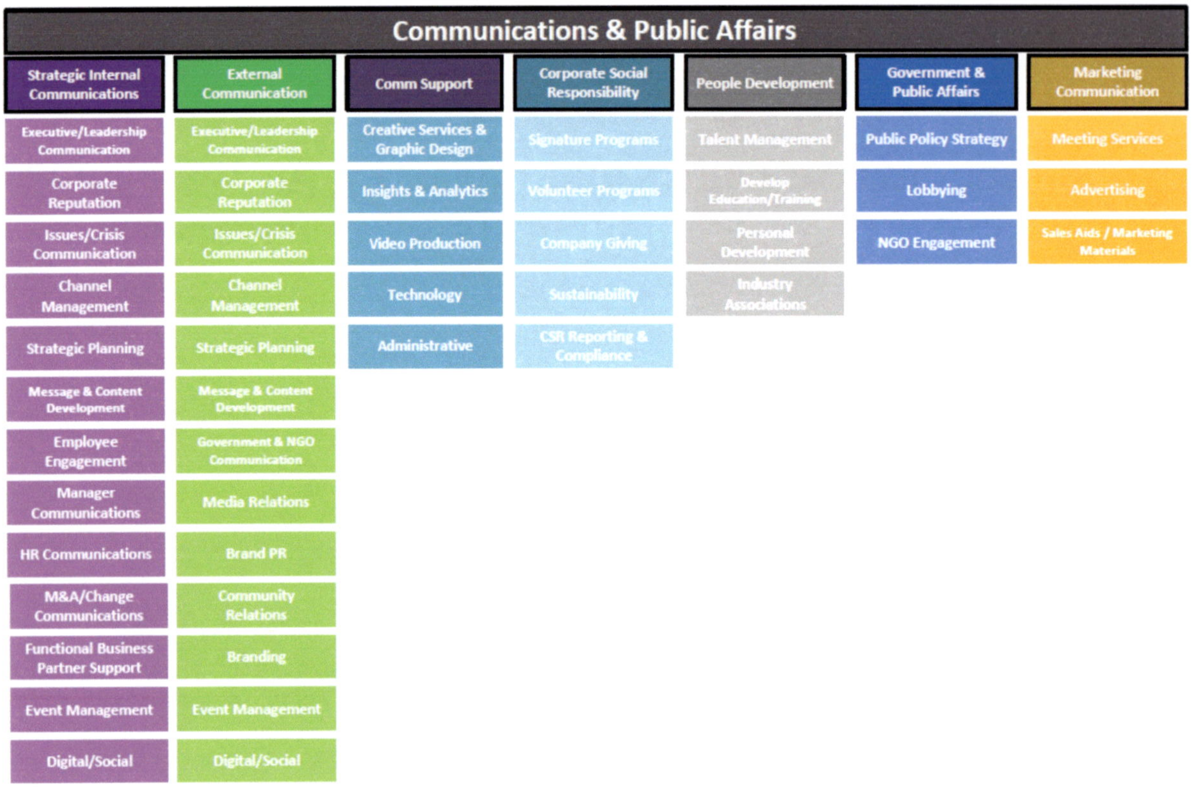

FIGURE 3-1 Organization of a typical corporate communications and public affairs office. SOURCE: Peter Debreceny, Gagen-MacDonald, "Strategic Internal Communications: The Current State." Courtesy of Gagen-MacDonald, copyright 2015.

Organizational Vision and Core Values

Several participants discussed the importance for an organization's vision and core values to be simple and universally understandable. Ms. Jennie Bledsoe, director of global internal communications for the Goodyear Tire & Rubber Company noted, as other participants had, the importance of emphasizing not only the *what* in communication but also the *why*.

As an example of the need to be flexible in communicating an organization's core values, Mr. William Power of Fleishman-Hillard described how IBM shifted its corporate image from that of a technology company, a builder of computers, to an "e-business," which means that "IBM understands business. We use internet technology as a tool to transform key business processes and help companies succeed."

Authenticity and Transparency in Communication

Several participants noted that trust is created through face-to-face communication that is both authentic and transparent. In an example of a company merger described by Dr. Hoey, managers helped to overcome resistance and fear on the part of employees by frequent contact ("managing by walking around"). Through frequent travel and teleconferences, they overcame the potential for misalignment of priorities between the two sets of executives. Mr. Debreceny recounted a merger between two companies in which the two communication teams merged to develop a communication strategy 6 months before the merger was publicly announced. Senior executives in both organizations led the strategy development. Ms. Bledsoe agreed with the frequently expressed commentary that the direct supervisor/manager—what Mr. Debreceny referred to as a "line-of-sight" manager—is "the critical link" between corporate and the employee.

"Leaders need to be open about being open," Dr. Hoey said. It is essential to be aware of the concerns of employees. "If you can't be transparent, at least be translucent," he advised. Identify key "influencers" not in the chain of command to help develop strategy, Dr. Hoey suggested. Ms. Wendi Strong noted that USAA's leaders meet with such influencers regularly to brief them on changes in management and policy. Mr. Ed Brill stated that one key to deep penetration of social media into IBM's overall communications is that it strives for transparency in corporate messaging—clarity about company policies and practices—something that has led to employee trust. An authentic voice combined with transparency is a huge corporate shift in internal communication, and it has produced employee trust, he said.

Dr. Vernon Miller, associate professor of communication at Michigan State University, focused on the best ways to maintain a high-reliability organization, such as the Air Force. His observations echoed many of the same ones made independently by the other communications experts at the workshop. For example, excellence requires fostering openness in message sending (disclosure) and receiving (receptivity to feedback) at all levels. In addition, passing along information and insight to one's direct reports is essential in hierarchical organizations. Regarding the negative external communications about which the Air Force is concerned, he said, "If you invite personnel to be engaged in their work, you must enable constructive, upward feedback. Action, receptivity to feedback, and giving feedback can thwart cynicism and malaise among personnel."

Like the other corporate presenters, Boeing's Mr. Ames described a largely "employee-centric" communication culture in which credibility on the part of management and respect for the employee are central. "Credibility is everyone's job," he said. "But communication is the first-line champion of it." However, Mr. Ames noted, one of the communication lessons that Boeing is learning is that "credibility with a diverse work force is a journey."

Organizational Strategy, Culture, and Structure

Participants discussed the importance of aligning strategy, culture, and structure within an organization and highlighted that an organization's behavior is as equally important as its communications. Part of the openness that is vital for a successful organization today, Dr. Miller said, is a willingness to discuss real strengths and weaknesses of key operations and processes regularly. He noted that the USAF selects intelligent, capable volunteers and introduces them to USAF core values through onboarding experiences in basic training. However, the most important period of value development, he said, may be during additional skill development training and in initial unit assignments, where the insights of experienced peers can reinforce or undermine the newcomer's individual development. In his view, "Organizations are always one generation away from extinction. The passing along of values and core knowledge is a necessity, not a luxury."

In his description of IBM's shifting its corporate image from computers to e-business, Mr. William Power related that it took a year to educate the workforce about what e-business means. Mr. Power noted that, as part of this education process, IBM conducts "jam sessions," a blog with a moderator that runs for 24 hours, allowing input from employees around the world. The name itself sounds invigorating and inviting to participants, he said. IBM's Mr. Brill added that the authentic voice his company has achieved derives from three things: (1) messages are often being written in the first person, (2) weaknesses are disclosed ("not everything is perfect"), and (3) the frequent inclusion of extraneous personal content imparts three-dimensionality.

While the fundamentals of communication have not changed, Mr. Debreceny said, there is a difference in the levels of energy and the placement of the emphasis. He pointed out that most of the emphasis now should be on "dialogue," but "transactional," "distribution," and "interactional" communication should still be pursued (see Figure 3-2).

Reaching the Audience

Mr. Debreceny began his presentation with the statement that 85 percent of all organizational digital communications today do not reach the intended recipient. In that context, Mr. Ryan Henary of FedEx Ground spoke

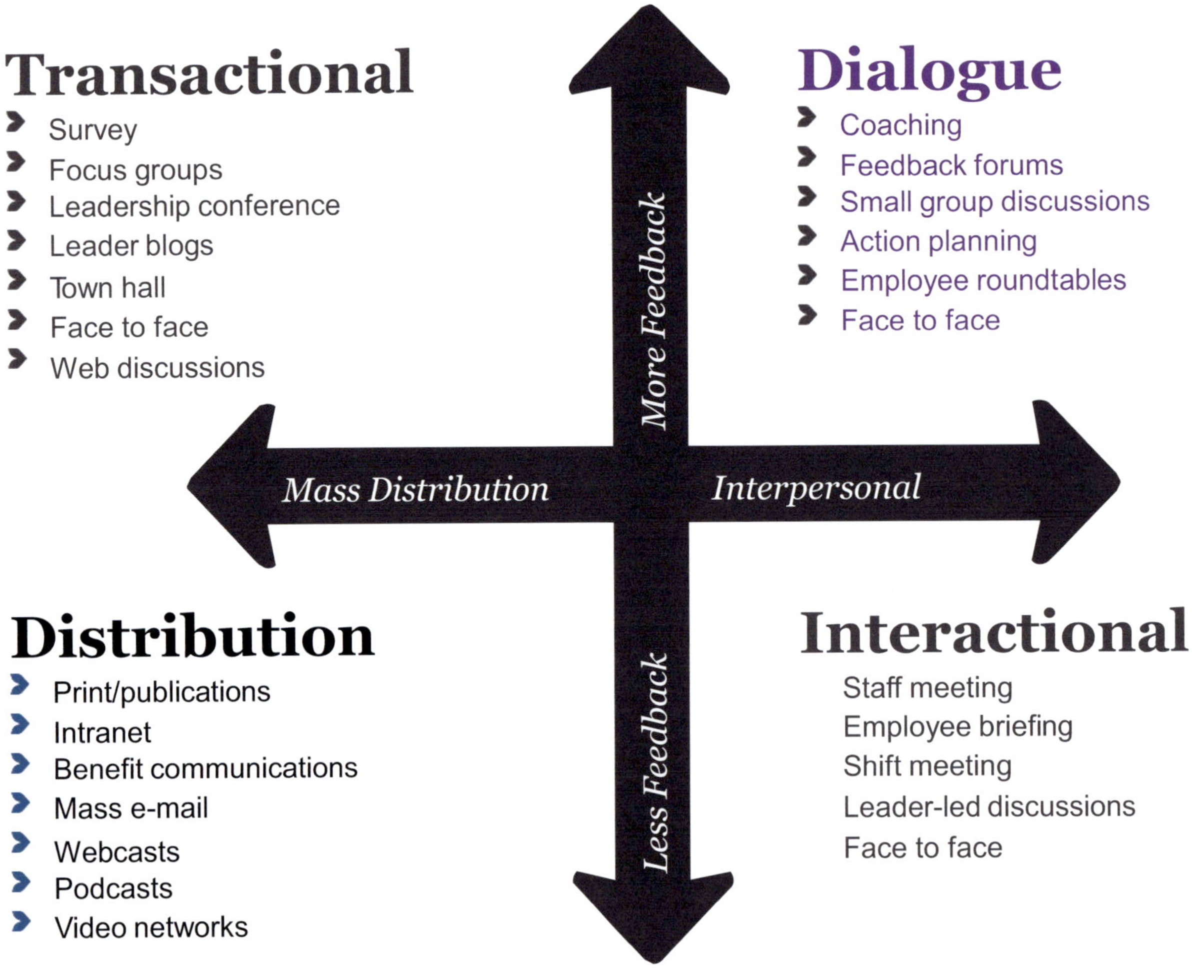

FIGURE 3-2 Elements of communication. SOURCE: Peter Debreceny, Gagen-MacDonald, "Strategic Internal Communications: The Current State." Courtesy of Gagen-MacDonald, copyright 2015.

about the importance of "tailored messaging": FedEx Ground tailors communications and tactics by audience, when appropriate. He also recommended asking people what they want to know and how they would like to receive the information—"keep it simple." A key to their communication strategy is that a simple, unifying message connects FedEx employees worldwide.

For internal social media, Goodyear uses a Microsoft program called Yammer. Because it is inside the company's firewall, Ms. Bledsoe said, it eased management's fears about communications potentially being too open. She commented that they addressed its implementation from both the management side and the employee side, giving guidelines to employees regarding what to post and not post and briefing senior managers on the program's security, uses, and value to the company. Yammer provides a full suite of measurement and analysis tools. The blog is moderated by her staff, and it can search for keywords and alert the moderators to violations of the guidelines. Anonymity is not allowed. Further, if the moderator deletes a post, then it is a "warm delete"; someone from management calls the poster, explains the problem, and helps the person reword the post.

In his presentation, which focused mainly on the use of social media in IBM, Mr. Brill shared four "key takeaways": (1) there is value in social media, (2) it should focus on objective outcomes, (3) a dedicated strategy is needed to drive adoption (in which authenticity matters), and (4) the best available communication technologies should be employed throughout the organization.

Communicating with Diverse Audiences

Several participants discussed the importance of tailoring communication channels to audience needs and expectations, both within and across generations. Ms. Bledsoe compared Goodyear's communication challenges to those of the Air Force: both have diverse employees from different generations at widely dispersed locations, and both use a range of communication tools and technologies to reach these employees. She described the tools that Goodyear currently uses to address these challenges. Among them is a mix of "high touch/high tech channels," including small-group meetings, toolkits and training for managers (with refreshers for those who display less engagement), a corporate intranet, internal social media, email, both plant and retail newsletters, and advocacy opportunities for their employees.

Maj. Gen. Mari Eder spoke about what she termed "The Millennial Air Force" and the need to "get beyond messaging to a two-way conversation that builds the Air Force narrative." She described a number of examples of the different ways in which this generation is fluent in communicating using social media and other technologies. For example, she presented that, as of February 2014, a survey showed that 55 percent of American Millennials reported having shared a "selfie" on social media. By contrast, 24 percent of Gen-X respondents had done so; 9 percent of Baby Boomers had; and only 4 percent of the Silent Generation (born before 1946) had shared a selfie. Connecting with peers in an authentic way is extremely important to this younger group, and they expect the same authenticity in communication with their employer.

Mr. Brill said that IBM is analogous to the Air Force in being a multi-pronged, global organization. It finds that about 10 percent of its workforce is active in internal digital communications, while only 3 to 4 percent (approximately 15,000 out of a total workforce of 400,000) is active in external digital communication. It sees that those employees who are most active in communicating are the most upwardly mobile and likely to succeed.

The Relationship Between Internal and External Communication

Participants noted that internal communications often escape organizational boundaries and become external communications. Mr. Debreceny stated that the industry communications environment is undergoing a revolution. The smartphone is the main conduit of this change, he said. Messages now come from the bottom up, rather than the top down—something that most top leaders find difficult to manage. Barriers between stakeholders and their audiences have all but disappeared. He agreed with the other presenters that, in this environment, transparency is essential to minimize the potential for misinformation and misinterpretation.

PUTTING SOCIAL MEDIA TO WORK FOR THE AIR FORCE

During discussions on the use of social media within the Air Force, several participants stated that there have been fundamental shifts away from the corporate (Air Force) "push" of information outward to a focus on the employees' (Airmen) "pull" for information and their own externalization of information, using social media.

Ms. Lois Kelly, chief executive officer of Foghound, presented the concept of the "threateningness" of social media to status, certainty, autonomy, relatedness, and fairness (SCARF)[1] in the military versus the external communication environment. The autonomy issue is particularly important, in her view. The distinction between "issuing information our way" and "sharing information with people" is crucial. Ms. Kelly noted that USAF social media use is missing the story of Air Power[2] advocacy, but is doing better with "team belongingness." Many participants agreed with Ms. Wendi Strong that it is best for management to admit up-front that "social media is scary," then

[1] Attributed to Dr. David Rock, *Your Brain at Work*, Harper Business, 2009.

[2] The Air Force Basic Doctrine Volume 1, updated February 27, 2015, defines "Air Power" as "the ability to project military power or influence through the control and exploitation of air, space, and cyberspace to achieve strategic, operational, or tactical objectives."

address what the threatening elements are and how the Air Force can manage them. The participants noted that the message to senior leadership should be, "We *have* to do this; so here is the best way to go about it."

Ms. Kelly noted that an organization needs professional analysts to interpret what social media communications mean to that organization. She described "use filters" as a way to prioritize and select which social media channel to use for different purposes. For example, one of the most important uses of social media is for dealing with a crisis (e.g., breaking news). Ms. Kelly said that Twitter is the best channel for use in these situations. She suggested using scenario planning for crisis situations to help stay in front of the story.

Goodyear's Ms. Bledsoe related that she had hired a young "reverse mentor" to explain the Millennial generation's views and communication practices to her. IBM's Mr. Brill described their "New2Blue" social community of new hires (mostly Millennials); the rest of IBM "watches" them online to learn about them as well as from them. Mr. Debreceny noted that IBM has encouraged every employee to become a social media advocate, but first one has to agree to undergo training. Mr. Brill said that his company has formal social computing guidelines that provide employees with both permission and direction for social communicating; and they all must take a 2-hour course every year to recertify for security issues. Mr. Ed Terpening of the Altimeter Group said that corporate training tends to focus on what *not* to do. He suggested that more guidance is needed for Airmen on "judgment training—that is, what they *can* do."

Mr. Terpening was asked, "How do you assess an organization's readiness for social media?" He replied that the starting point is research. They take diagnostic information and put it into the context of the client, often using case studies. Gen. Douglas Fraser commented that this is not unlike introducing any new program—there is a need for change in management, training, and guidance.

The committee asked, "What does a successful strategy look like?' Ms. Kelly replied that there are three things to know and do:

1. Identify the desired outcomes in terms of perception and behavioral goals. How do you communicate in new ways to affect perception and behavioral goals using social media?
2. Build a "predictive analytics capability" based on measurement that uses analyses of past and current use trends on a specific social media platform to forecast future use patterns.
3. Consider the complexity of new technologies. Internal communication based on social media "needs to be easy, blessed with authority . . . and there are privacy issues."

Ms. Strong noted that one of the true benefits of social media is that it can be measured—real time—using analytical tools. Soon, most organizations will be able to use these "analytics" and social media metrics in a predictive way. Gen. Fraser commented that analytics remove the fear that "I'm not able to control my message as I go into social media." Accenture Digital's Mr. Robert Harles added that the predictive element not only helps keep the organization safe, but also tells leadership what they need to know in order to achieve the desired outcomes. It tells them how to fit the message into what decision makers and influencers are thinking, as well as how they are obtaining and using information.

Mr. Harles suggested thinking about social media not only as communication, but also as a strategic element, "allowing you to understand the things going on around you, understand the people you need to recruit, and in general understand how Air Force people are getting their information and using it." Benefits can be unexpected. For example, Mr. Brill reported that at IBM they find that those employees more actively engaged in internal social media are the best innovators and are "120 percent" more likely to generate innovation.

Gen. Fraser summarized this part of the discussion: "Social media with predictive analytics will give me the information I need to understand the world in which I'm trying to navigate. Without it, I'm flying blind. " Mr. Harles added, "You can't *not* do this. It's going to happen—and already is—whether you get involved in it or not. You need to build the social enterprise into the organization and make it strategic" (see Figure 3-3).

Mr. Terpening described six stages of "social business transformation" (Figure 3-4). His assessment is that the Air Force is somewhere in the "engagement" stage, working toward the "formalized" and "strategic" levels.

Figure 3-5 describes ways of measuring the six stages. In Mr. Terpening's view, the Air Force meets the requirements shown in green, at least for the current level of maturity. It partially meets the requirements indicated

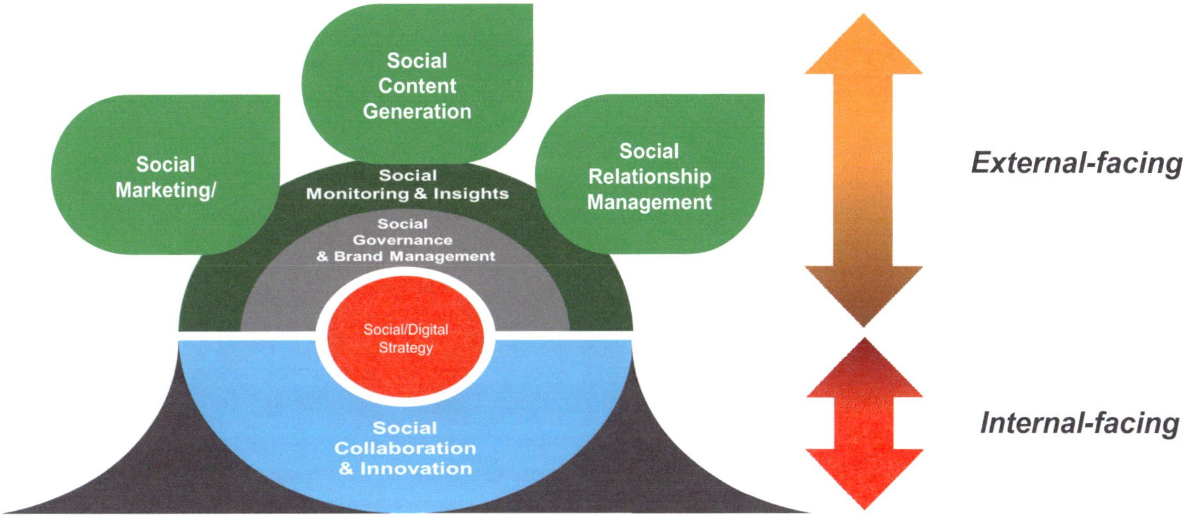

FIGURE 3-3 Embedding social media into an organization. SOURCE: Robert Harles, Social & Collaboration, Accenture Interactive, "Building the Social Enterprise: US Air Force." Courtesy of Accenture Interactive.

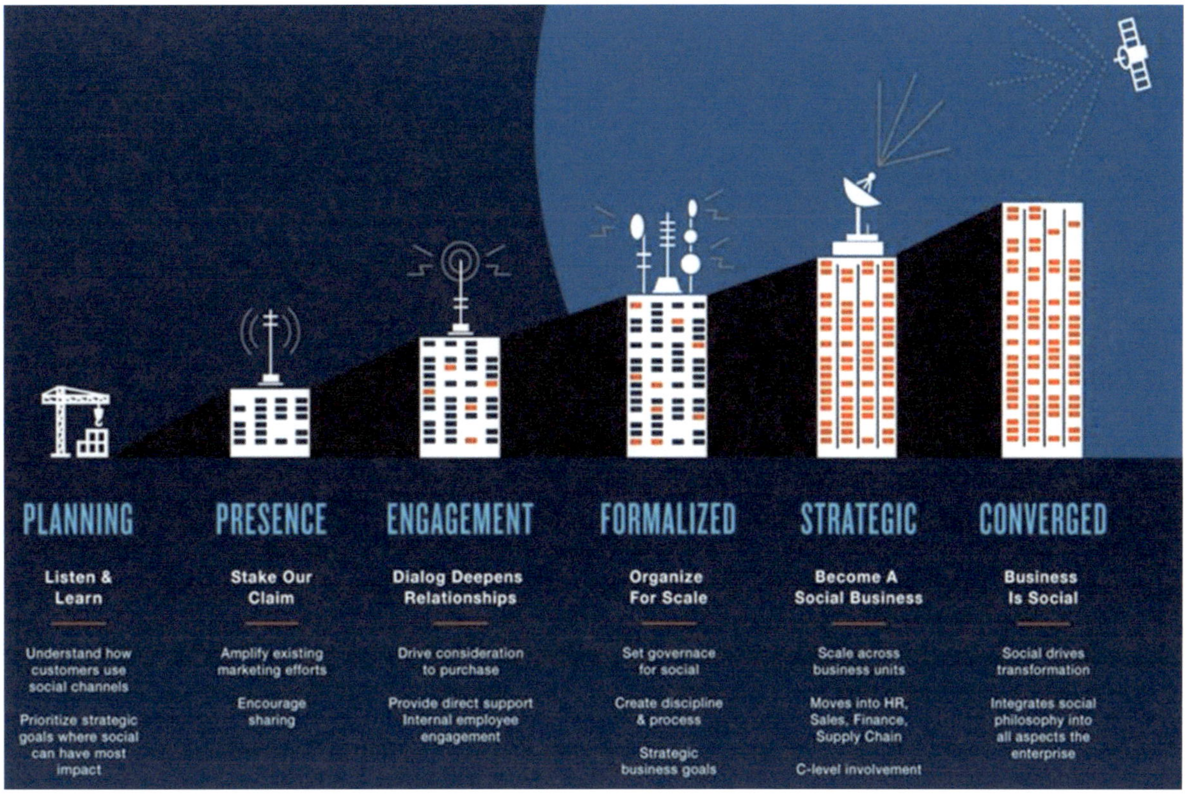

FIGURE 3-4 Stages in the transformation of an organization and integration of social media. SOURCE: Ed Terpening, Industry Analyst, Altimeter Group, "Social Media Industry Research & Insights to Inform Advanced USAF Strategy." Courtesy of Altimeter Group, copyright 2015.

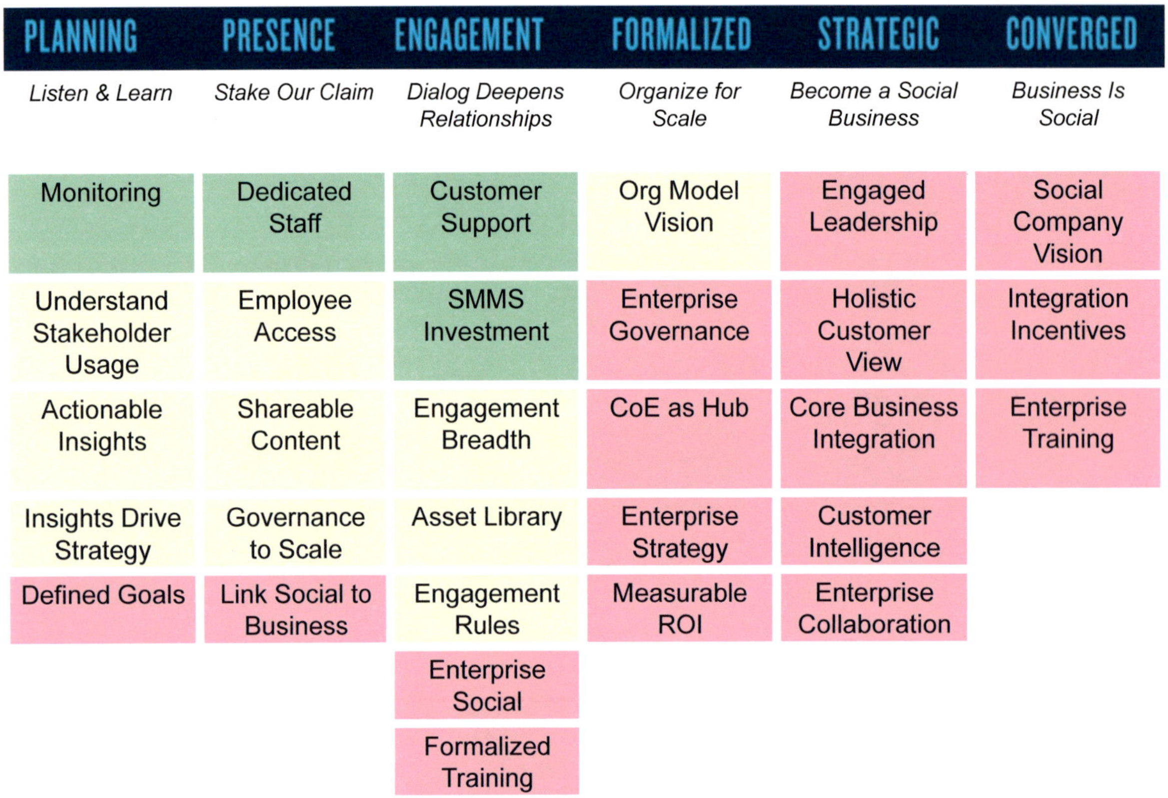

FIGURE 3-5 Six stage maturity and readiness approach to measuring organizational progress toward implementing social media. SOURCE: Ed Terpening, Industry Analyst, Altimeter Group, "Social Media Industry Research & Insights to Inform Advanced USAF Strategy." Courtesy of Altimeter Group, copyright 2015.

in yellow, but more work is needed there. Those shown in red need significant attention, he said. Brig. Gen. Kathleen Cook agreed that the Air Force is currently in a transition phase in dealing with social media. It was noted by several participants that an organization does not need to be at the highest level of maturity and instead should determine the appropriate maturity level based on the needs of, and benefits to, the organization.

Mr. Terpening's company prescribes a variety of different social media organizational strategies for different organizations, depending on structure, operations, and needs. For the Air Force, he suggests a "hub-and-spoke" approach (see Figure 3-6). This model is succeeding best for most organizations, he said. In it, a cross-functional team sits in a centralized position and aids various organizational nodes and activities, with all units and all personnel being linked to the USAF social media network.

Many workshop participants recognized that social media will not solve all of the Air Force's communication problems; however, they are potentially effective tools that have been underutilized. Many of them stated that for greatest effect, social media should be customized to meet the Air Force's culture and specific needs and implemented in a carefully planned way, utilizing its powerful built-in analytics capabilities, with involvement and oversight by Air Force senior leadership.

Gen. Fraser summarized his reactions to the information presented at the workshop as follows: "The workshop changed my perspective on the value of social media use in an organization—when integrated through a deliberate communications strategy—for enhancing internal communication, for improving workforce collaboration, and for enhancing an organization's performance."

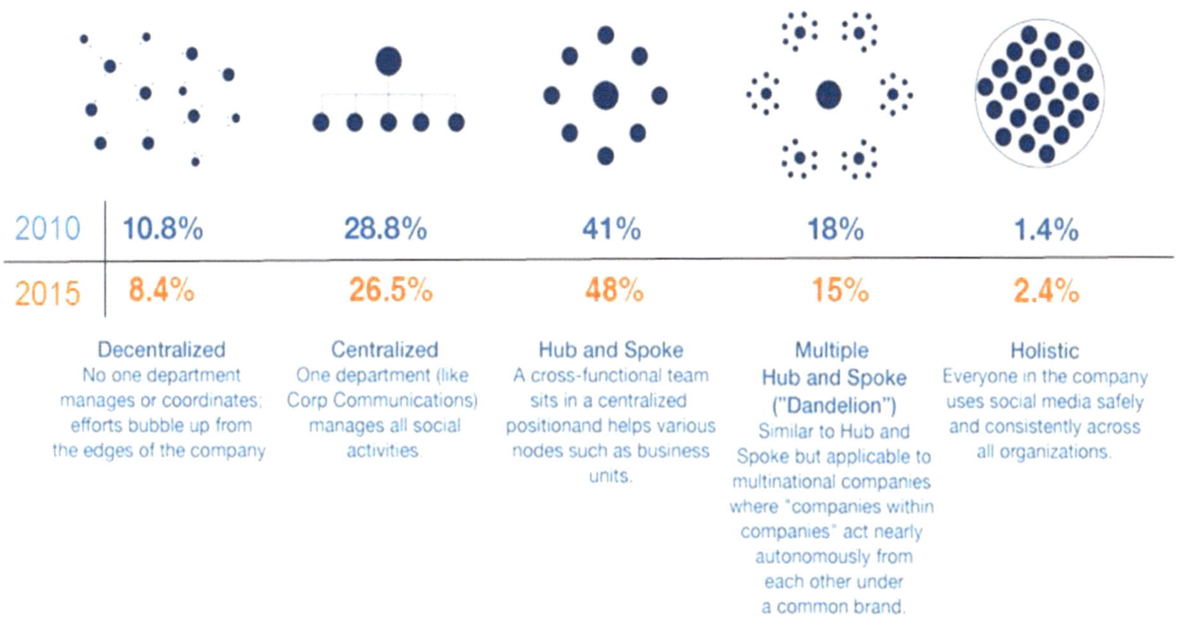

FIGURE 3-6 Various organizational models for managing social media. SOURCE: Ed Terpening, Industry Analyst, Altimeter Group, "Social Media Industry Research & Insights to Inform Advanced USAF Strategy." Courtesy of Altimeter Group, copyright 2015.

Theme 8—Role of Social Media in the Air Force. As noted by Gen. Cook, the USAF does not have a clear policy toward the use of social media, and its use of social media is thus far limited. Many participants noted that internally, social media should be available to all employees to help create a sense of community and connectedness across the diversity of the Air Force while facilitating many core Air Force functions. Externally, they are seen as essential tools for communicating with all audiences and can provide early warning, through analytics, regarding emerging issues and potential conflicts. As Gen. Fraser commented, social media and analytics together can provide the "radar" into the Air Force's "organizational battlespace" for both internal and external communications. For companies such as IBM, social media have been a driver of innovation. Several participants noted that corporate experience has shown that there will be resistance on the part of senior leadership, but it is essential to engage fully with this new communications reality. Experience has also shown that awareness of the benefits, through training and "reverse mentorship" of senior leaders, will overcome the hesitancy. Formal guidelines and training on what can and cannot be done can reduce the risk of misuse.

POSSIBLE OPTIONS FOR THE USAF IN ORGANIZATION AND PROCESSES

The workshop presentations and discussion with top professional communicators showed that the communication environment within the Air Force has changed in recent years. As Dr. Pamela Drew stated, "There has been a massive shift from the 'broadcast/push' corporate-organizational viewpoint to the employee or Airman-centric viewpoint. It has decentralized command and is self-replicating." Ms. Deborah Westphal said that this is a struggle between control of the message and learning how to live in an environment where there is no control. The challenge, as Dr. Drew pointed out, is to harness that energy through training and, in particular, through the development of a culture of authentic, transparent communication.

Gen. Fraser added "It's not the people themselves that we've lost control of; it's information. We have to get comfortable with trusting our people to be our best 'ambassadors.'" He said there is still a chain of command and people are still accountable to the organization, even though they are now passing information along in whatever way they choose to transmit it. Dr. Drew said that adopting a new approach to communication will work "if you set the rules—that is, 'If you embarrass the organization you will face consequences.'"

As was repeatedly emphasized by several participants during the workshop, the key management issue with respect to Air Force communication today is that leaders and supervisors need to "take ownership" of communication in all its forms. Leadership, at all levels, matters in enhancing communication.

To give Airmen the information they want regarding policies and decisions, Dr. Hoey recommended providing supervisors and managers with a toolkit—a complete package with briefing materials and other relevant information. However, cautioned Mr. Debreceny, top-level communications require "translation"; they need to be adapted to the user.

As noted previously by some participants, for corporations similar in complexity to the USAF, the responsibility for both internal and external communication is most often held centrally. Execution of communications can occur in a decentralized manner, but only if there is a single point of governance and integration at the highest level. Additionally, many of the participants from industry and academia expressed the view that communications leadership should have a seat at the most senior-level tables and hold senior-level positions commensurate with those of other essential functions.

Lastly, several participants presented information on staffing levels assigned to communication activities. For example, research conducted by Mr. Terpening's company, Altimeter Group, showed that corporations with more than 50,000 employees typically have about 20 staff assigned to social media alone. Most participants stated that the Air Force communications organization needs to be modernized in terms of organizational structure, processes, and tools and sufficiently staffed and resourced to carry out its modernized functions.

4

Measuring Communication Effectiveness Across Diverse Backgrounds and Missions

As with any program, measuring the effectiveness of communication is vital to understanding its value and learning how to shape it for greater effectiveness.

Brig. Gen. Kathleen Cook expressed to the committee a desire for definable, measurable, results-based outcomes, using the approach that "we are trying to change the knowledge, attitudes, or beliefs of a specific audience to achieve a specific action." This clarity, she said, would not only inform the message, but also provide a construct under which to align the U.S. Air Force's (USAF's) weight of effort and inform *what* they should be measuring themselves against.

DEFINING "EFFECTIVE COMMUNICATION" IN THE AIR FORCE CONTEXT

What is "effective" communication? Akin to weapons deployment, it can be described as communication that reaches its target, impacts its audience, and achieves the intended objective for that particular audience. Several participants stated that whether in the context of an individual message or an Air Force-wide communication strategy, this requires setting objectives, planning, and acting in a deliberate and organized fashion.

The discussion among several of the workshop participants highlighted that in the process of planning the elements of a communication strategy, leadership should first define what they hope to achieve. These participants acknowledged that communication requires measurement, and the selected measures must be specific, measurable, attainable, relevant, and timely. To that end, they noted, leadership needs a clear and consistent vision of what success looks like; this vision of success should be tied to goals.

Ms. Katie Paine, chief executive officer of Paine Publishing, established the context for discussing this topic at the workshop by summarizing the Barcelona Principles, a set of industry standards for measuring communications effectiveness and outcomes, developed by an assembly of communication-measurement professionals in Spain.[1] A few workshop participants discussed that an Air Force communication "baseline" could be defined as instituting within the communication culture a sense that the Air Force must measure its communications in order to understand their outcomes clearly.

[1] For more information on the standards, see Paine Publishing, "Standards Central," http://www.painepublishing.com/standards-central, accessed October 5, 2015.

MEASURES OF EFFECTIVENESS AND SUCCESS

Ms. Paine described six steps to achieving a quality of measurement that complies with the Barcelona Principals:

1. *Define your goals*—Identify the role of communication in reaching the goal, defining the activity metrics (e.g., percentage increase in visits to AF.mil), and determining the outcome metrics (e.g., percentage growth in program funding or recruits) in terms of the mission.
2. *Understanding stakeholders*—"Connect the dots" between stakeholders, prioritize them, and understand their need and interests.
3. *Define your benchmarks*—Compare past performance over time or compare results with those of other services. The most important entity to measure against, Ms. Paine said, is "whatever keeps the generals up at night."
4. *Define your metrics*—Pick the right metric. The ideal index is actionable, is there when you need it, continuously improves your processes, and gets the results you need.
5. *Select data collection tools*—Select the right tool(s) depending on what you are measuring.
6. *Use the data to make better decisions*—Ask "So what?" three times, in order to understand what the data actually mean in real-world terms.

Ms. Wendi Strong asked how one might measure messages in advance (i.e., pre-launch testing). Ms. Paine recommended focus-group studies around the country for this purpose.

Col. Sean Monogue asked how one measures trust. Ms. Paine replied that it is mainly done with surveys. Turning the survey into a game is a useful technique, she said, because it fits with the gaming proclivities of today's employees. It tests institutional knowledge in a way that makes the survey fun.

AVAILABLE ANALYTICAL TOOLS AND METHODS

A variety of specific tools and techniques used to measure communication effectiveness were presented and discussed. The appropriate tool depends on the objective:

- Content analysis can be used to evaluate messaging, positioning, themes, or sentiment.
- Survey research can be used to measure awareness, perception, relationships, or preference.
- Web analytics can be used to measure engagement, action, or purchases.

As one example, Mr. Ed Brill said that IBM conducts a biennial "climate survey" of its employees. It finds considerable ambiguity in views of what IBM is. He said that, in contrast to the Air Force, lower-level employees tend to report that they have more information about IBM than managers do.

Tools also exist for mapping social networks and analyzing activities in social media. Ms. Paine described a method for measuring engagement with social media. Additionally, Foghound's Ms. Lois Kelly had pointed out the need for a "predictive analytics capability" for measuring social media (see discussion in Chapter 3). Lastly, Mr. Robert Harles described technically sophisticated techniques for monitoring social media use and analyzing engagement, which together can form a "social media radar" for predictive capability.

KEY CONSIDERATIONS

In Mr. Harles' view, setting measurable goals up front is critical—that is, how do you drive strategic impact? For example, he suggested focusing less on building large numbers of followers and more on building meaningful relationships with those who contribute valuable insight or influence others toward achieving stated objectives.

Ms. Paine said that it is essential not only to agree on metrics of success, as defined by senior leadership, but also to then tie rewards to them. In business, bonuses and salaries are tied to measurable outcomes.

A key role of employee feedback surveys, she continued, is to ascertain whether employees are able to connect their roles directly back to the corporate vision; the surveys should reveal whether the communication strategy is resulting in a culture of communication. Ms. Paine stated that value must be measured in real terms. In other words, data on reach, engagement, and impressions are less important than driving actionable insights, changing user behaviors, or influencing policy and strategic outcomes.

Several participants noted that the point of measuring communication is to have a basis on which to take action. For example, such data might allow the Air Force to determine the best way to deal with crises by overcoming negative or extraneous external communications. They can help determine what internal or external information is being used effectively and what is not. With these tools, the Air Force can use the data to inform important decisions. However, as Mr. Harles noted, "When you have all the analytics, you still have to synthesize that information"—or, as Ms. Paine put it, "Research without insight is just trivia."

Theme 9—Measurement. Several measurement experts presented established tools and techniques for measuring the effectiveness of communication in an organization. As discussed, the process begins with senior leadership setting goals and determining desired outcomes—not simply outputs. Communication excellence can then be measured against quantifiable objectives and resulting performance, and the data can be used to improve decision making. Measuring social media use and analyzing how employees are communicating provides important awareness of the communication networks and key influencers within the organization. There are experts in industry who guide organizations in confidently and effectively planning and implementing a well-integrated communication strategy using the best available tools.

5

Restatement of Main Themes

Culture of Communication. Many participants expressed the view that the U.S. Air Force (USAF) lacks a "culture of communication"—a culture where every leader/supervisor is responsible and accountable for communicating within the organization. Based on several participants' statements, senior leaders do not "own" communication as an essential part of Air Force operations—that is, they do not integrate it into the overall Air Force strategy. Consequently, there is no real commitment to messaging internally or externally in a consistent and deliberate way. Infusing a culture of communication throughout the Air Force would mean that communication is free flowing within the organization and understood as everyone's responsibility, for which leaders are accountable. Such a culture is built on a foundation of trust at the Airman level. Trust, in turn, is best cultivated through communications that are authentic and transparent, conveyed with a human and personal voice, with a realistic context and a focus on the "Why?" Ultimately, actions matter more than words, and the two have to be closely aligned and integrated in order to maintain the trust of highly "connected" and aware Airmen. Trust is a two-way street; in such a culture, every participant feels a responsibility to protect the reputation of the organization.

Organizational Responsibility. Several participants noted that Air Force communication leadership currently do not have frequent or reliable access to senior leaders and executive-level meetings, or hold senior positions commensurate with other core functions of the Air Force such as personnel or operations. As highlighted by some presenters, given the lack of integration and access, the USAF Public Affairs (PA) office is often assigned responsibility for tasks that it does not have the authority or sufficient resources to execute efficiently, while other important functions are unassigned and not performed. These participants additionally highlighted the importance of having adequate resources for planning, execution, and measurement within an organization.

Communication Strategy. As discussed between the participants from the USAF and several participants from industry, the USAF does not have a coherent communication strategy encompassing both internal and external communication and the diverse audiences it must engage. As a result, there is not one, clear set of organizational objectives owned by the senior-most leadership. Responsibility for external communication is divided between the PA office (for media) and the Air Force Recruiting Command (for recruiting). Internal communication is stovepiped at the operational command level, where it is ad hoc, subject specific, and disconnected from the Airmen work-force. Several other participants noted that, in general, a communication strategy should improve the performance of an organization and contain outcome-oriented goals tailored to specific audiences. Additionally, they noted that an effective communication strategy is centrally owned and governed with decentralized execution—focused on desired outcomes and impact, not just education and information.

Brand. Several participants compared the USAF with the other military services and noted that the USAF does not have a single, clear, and compelling unifying theme or message—a brand—especially one that is closely aligned both internally and externally. This is partly a function of the diverse domains and complex multiple missions of the Air Force, and partly a function of its high-tech nature. As several other participants noted, a brand need not encompass every aspect of the Air Force's mission, but it should reflect the essence of the Air Force in a way that "Aim High . . . Fly, Fight, Win" does not. Additionally, they noted, messages can be tailored to different audiences and tied back to the single unifying theme, or brand, in order to inspire, inform, and remain emotionally relevant.

Internal Communication. As noted by Peter Debreceny, internal communications in large organizations have become more important than official external communications; but several other workshop participants voiced the view that the USAF has not adequately addressed this shift in emphasis. Airmen by and large understand what the Air Force is and does. However, they are narrowly focused on their job, communicate most often with their immediate cohorts, and often do not understand the connection between their work and the larger purpose and mission of the Air Force. Their connection to Air Force policy and purpose is primarily face-to-face, through their supervisor—and this continues to be the most trusted and effective form of communication. However, as discussed by some of the participants, supervisors often do not realize the implications of policies on their unit's work and consequently do not communicate that clearly to the workforce. As a result, Airmens' communications among themselves and with their networks via social media are unmanaged and sometimes appear to be unjustifiably negative. Communications "up" as well as outward from the workforce to the public are increasingly important compared to traditional communication down through the chain of command. As discussed by Brian Hoey, involving internal "influencers" outside the chain of command in the communication process is one method that companies have used to facilitate stronger internal messaging.

External Communication. Several participants noted that, as was shown through examples in other organizations, internal and external communications increasingly overlap and merge. Because of the pervasive use of social media, there are no longer boundaries between the two. These participants additionally noted that Airmen are potentially the best and most direct channel for positive communication with external as well as internal audiences, and the best advocates for the Air Force with the public. While discussing issues in describing the value of the USAF, several participants expressed the view that a powerful way to tell the Air Force story, both internally and externally, is through the use of "storytelling" involving Air Force people doing interesting or even extraordinary, "heroic" things. Graphics are becoming more effective than words, and words should be minimized to reduce messages to their essence.

General Role of Social Media. The social media experts participating in the workshop stated that social media are no longer separate and distinct from mainstream communication; they have become an integral part of the communication ecosystem and are a main component of communication at all levels today, for business as well as for personal use, to build networks and to strengthen collaborative problem-solving. In many large companies, social media are no longer seen as peripheral or optional, but as core functions. Social analytic tools and technologies have developed to a degree of sophistication such that they can now be used to gain real-time insight into communications effectiveness.

Role of Social Media in the Air Force. As noted by Brig. Gen. Kathleen Cook, the USAF does not have a clear policy toward the use of social media, and its use of social media is thus far limited. Many participants noted that internally, social media should be available to all employees to help create a sense of community and connectedness across the diversity of the Air Force while facilitating many core Air Force functions. Externally, they are seen as essential tools for communicating with all audiences and can provide early warning, through analytics, regarding emerging issues and potential conflicts. As Gen. Douglas Fraser commented, social media and analytics together can provide the "radar" into the Air Force's "organizational battlespace" for both internal and external communications. For companies such as IBM, social media have been a driver of innovation. Several participants noted that corporate experience has shown that there will be resistance on the part of senior leadership, but it is essential to engage fully with this new communications reality. Experience has also shown that awareness of the benefits, through training and "reverse mentorship" of senior leaders, will overcome the hesitancy. Formal guidelines and training on what can and cannot be done can reduce the risk of misuse.

Measurement. Several measurement experts presented established tools and techniques for measuring the effectiveness of communication in an organization. As discussed, the process begins with senior leadership setting goals and determining desired outcomes—not simply outputs. Communication excellence can then be measured against quantifiable objectives and resulting performance, and the data can be used to improve decision making. Measuring social media use and analyzing how employees are communicating provides important awareness of the communication networks and key influencers within the organization. There are experts in industry who guide organizations in confidently and effectively planning and implementing a well-integrated communication strategy using the best available tools.

Appendixes

A

Biographical Sketches of Committee Members

GENERAL DOUGLAS M. FRASER, *Chair*, retired from the U.S. Air Force (USAF) in January 2013 after a 37-year career. Since retiring, Gen. Fraser works as a global security consultant with several U.S. defense companies and is the principal of Doug Fraser, LLC. His last assignment in the U.S. armed forces was as the Commander, U.S. Southern Command, responsible for U.S. military operations in Central and South America and the Caribbean. In this capacity, Gen. Fraser was responsible for leading Department of Defense relief efforts following the 2010 Haiti earthquake. Prior to commanding U.S. Southern Command, he served as the Deputy Commander, U.S. Pacific Command from 2008-2009. Gen. Fraser commanded operational flying units across the U.S. Air Force at the squadron, group, and wing levels. As a general officer, in addition to U.S. Southern Command, he commanded the U.S. Air Force Space Warfare Center and four different organizations in Alaska: Alaskan Command, the Alaskan North American Defense Region, Joint Task Force Alaska, and Eleventh Air Force. Gen. Fraser's staff assignments include two tours in the Pentagon, the first in Headquarters U.S. Air Force and the second in the Office of the Assistant Secretary of Defense for Strategy, Resources, and Requirements. He also served on the staff at Headquarters, U.S. Pacific Command and at Headquarters, U.S. Air Force Space Command. He holds a bachelor's degree in political science from the U.S. Air Force Academy and a master's degree in political science from Auburn University at Montgomery. He is also a graduate of the USAF Weapons School, Squadron Officer School, Air Command and Staff College, and the National War College. He is a command pilot with more than 3,300 flying hours in the F-15, F-15E, F-16, and the C-37.

PAMELA A. DREW, *Vice Chair*. is chief executive officer of Premier Aerospace and Defense, a provider of advisory services in global aerospace, defense, and information solutions. In her 28-year career, Dr. Drew has served as a senior executive for several top-tier aerospace and defense firms, including Boeing, Northrop Grumman, TASC, and Exelis. In her various roles, she has led large-scale businesses providing mission-critical solutions to the Department of Defense, the Department of Homeland Security, the Federal Aviation Administration, NASA, the Intelligence Community, and portions of the global commercial aviation sector. Dr. Drew has held several leadership roles with National Research Council boards and committees, including as the vice chair of the Air Force Studies Board and on the "NextGen" Air Traffic Management committee for the Transportation Research Board. She also serves on the board of directors for the University of Washington's Applied Physics Laboratory. Dr. Drew has been named an associate fellow of the American Institute of Aeronautics and Astronautics. She also serves on the Strategic Advisory Councils to the Chancellor and Dean of Engineering at the University of Colorado, Boulder, where she earned her Ph.D. in computer science.

RICHARD P. HALLION is a senior advisor to the Science and Technology Policy Institute. Dr. Hallion received his B.A. and Ph.D. in history from the University of Maryland. He also graduated from executive training programs at the Federal Executive Institute and the Kennedy School of Government, Harvard University. He has been a curator at the National Air and Space Museum, Smithsonian Institution; a historian with NASA and the U.S. Air Force; policy analyst for the Secretary of the Air Force; senior advisor for air and space issues, for the Air Force's Directorate for Security, Counterintelligence, and Special Programs; and special advisor for aerospace technology for the Air Force Chief Scientist. He also serves as a research associate in aeronautics for the National Air and Space Museum and is a member of the board of trustees of Florida Polytechnic University. He is a fellow of the American Institute of Aeronautics and Astronautics, a fellow of the Royal Aeronautical Society, and a fellow of the Royal Historical Society.

JOANN KEYTON is professor of communication at North Carolina State University. She specializes in group communication and organizational communication. Her current research examines the collaborative processes and relational aspects of interdisciplinary teams, participants' use of language in team meetings, the multiplicity of cultures in organizations, and how messages are manipulated in sexual harassment. Her research is field focused, and she was honored with the 2011 Gerald Phillips Award for Distinguished Applied Communication Scholarship by the National Communication Association. Her research has been published in *Business Communication Quarterly*, *Communication Studies*, *Communication Theory*, *Communication Yearbook*, *Journal of Applied Communication Research*, *Journal of Business Communication*, *Management Communication Quarterly*, *Small Group Research*, *Southern Communication Journal*, and numerous edited collections including the *Handbook of Group Communication Theory and Research*, *The SAGE Handbook of Organizational Communication*, and *The Oxford Handbook of Organizational Climate and Culture*. In addition to publications in scholarly journals and edited collections, she has published three textbooks for courses in group communication, research methods, and organizational culture in addition to co-editing an organizational communication case book. Dr. Keyton was editor of the *Journal of Applied Communication Research*, Volumes 31-33, and founding editor of *Communication Currents*, Volumes 1-5. Currently, she is editor of *Small Group Research*. She is a founder and vice-chair of the Interdisciplinary Network for Group Research.

WENDI E. STRONG is executive vice president of Enterprise Affairs and chief communications officer of USAA, one of America's leading financial services companies. USAA has proudly served the military community since 1922 and has become well known for its exceptional customer service, financial strength, and work environment. USAA offers its more than 11 million members a full range of insurance, banking, investment products, and financial advice designed to help them achieve financial security. Headquartered in San Antonio, Texas, with more than 27,000 employees in offices throughout the United States and Europe, USAA owns and manages assets of nearly $213 billion. Ms. Strong leads the association's strategic communications functions and has responsibility for corporate and CEO communications, reputation management, corporate responsibility, and community and military affairs. Her team is focused on engaging and building lasting relationships with USAA's constituents. Prior to joining USAA in 2000, Ms. Strong served as vice president of strategic communications for Associates First Capital Corporation and in executive leadership roles at Kimberly-Clark Corporation and Rosewood Hotels and Resorts. In addition to her 30 years of corporate experience, she spent 6 years as a public relations executive at Hill+Knowlton and Dallas-based Holt & Associates. Ms. Strong has many active and past board and professional memberships to include the following: member and board of trustees of the Arthur W. Page Society; board of trustees for the Institute of Public Relations; member of the Public Relations Society of America; member of The Wisemen; and member of the advisory board for the Mayborn School of Journalism at the University of North Texas.

B

Workshop Statement of Task

An ad hoc committee will plan and conduct a 3-day interactive, multidisciplinary public workshop that focuses on addressing the underlying challenges inherent in developing and evaluating an effective communication strategy for Air Force leadership. During the workshop, participants will be asked to discuss options for how best to describe the complexity of the Air Force mission to a wide spectrum of audiences to include recent high school graduates as well as soon to retire Airmen. It is anticipated that the workshop will help to define a baseline for measuring effective communication within the Air Force as well as to explore ideas on how to best communicate with each generation of Air Force personnel, to include: millennials, generation X, baby boomers, and the silent generation. Finally, the workshop will identify possible options for new organizational processes that could enhance communication effectiveness as well as discussing the analytical tools and methods that are available for evaluating communication effectiveness. The committee will plan and organize the workshop, select and invite speakers and discussants, and moderate the discussions. A committee-authored workshop report will be prepared in accordance with institutional guidelines.

C

Workshop Participants

COMMITTEE MEMBERS

Gen. Douglas M. Fraser (U.S. Air Force, Ret.), *Chair*
Dr. Pamela A. Drew, Premier Aerospace and Defense, *Vice Chair*
Dr. Richard P. Hallion, Science and Technology Policy Institute
Dr. Joann Keyton, North Carolina State University
Ms. Wendi Strong, USAA

AIR FORCE STUDIES BOARD STAFF

Dr. Joan Fuller, Director
Mr. Andrew Kreeger, Program Officer
Ms. Dionna Ali, Research Assistant
Ms. Marguerite Schneider, Administrative Coordinator
Mr. Courtland Lewis, Consultant

SPEAKERS

Mr. Brian R. Ames, Vice President, Employee Communications, Boeing Company
Ms. Jennie Bledsoe, Director, Global Internal Communications, Goodyear Tire & Rubber Company
Mr. Ed Brill, Vice President, Social Business Cloud Services, Office of the CIO, IBM
Brig. Gen. Kathleen Cook, Director of Air Force Public Affairs, U.S. Air Force
Mr. Peter Debreceny, Senior Partner, Gagen-MacDonald
Maj. Gen. (U.S. Army, Ret.) Mari Eder, President, Benson's Review, LLC
Mr. Robert Harles, Managing Director and Global Lead, Social Media and Collaboration, Accenture Digital
Mr. Ryan Henary, Managing Director, Internal Communications, FedEx Ground
Dr. Brian Hoey, Principal, Hoey Group
Capt. Samuel Hubbard, ACC/A5A10
Ms. Lois Kelly, Founder and CEO, Foghound
Lt. Gen. Steven L. Kwast, Commander and President, Air University, Maxwell Air Force Base

Dr. Vernon Miller, Associate Professor, Michigan State University
Ms. Katie Paine, Founder and CEO, Paine Publishing, LLC
HON F. Whitten Peters, Partner William & Connolly, LLP, and Former Secretary of the U.S. Air Force
Mr. William Power, Senior Partner and Senior Vice President Global Practice Leader, Brand Marketing, Fleishman-Hillard
HON James Roche, Former Secretary of U.S. Air Force
Mr. Ed Terpening, Industry Analyst, Altimeter Group
Dr. Alan Vick, Senior Political Scientist, RAND Corporation
Gen. Mark A. Welsh III, Chief of Staff, U.S. Air Force

ADDITIONAL PARTICIPANTS

Ms. Laura Cooney, Program Analyst, Air Force Office of Scientific Research
Ms. Erin Krayer, Digital Outreach, Air Force Office of Scientific Research
Ms. Molly Lachance, Program Analyst Communications and Outreach, Air Force Office of Scientific Research
Dr. Mark Lewis, Director, Science and Technology Policy Institute
Ms. Vicki Looney, EVP for Business Development, Aspeyre Group
Ms. Rebecca Miller, Policy Fellow, Science and Technology Policy Institute
Col. Sean Monogue, Chief for Strategy and Assessments, Office of Public Affairs, U.S. Air Force
Mr. Jeffrey Stanley, Associate Deputy Director (Science, Technology & Engineering), U.S. Air Force
Ms. Deborah Westphal, CEO, Toffler Associates
Ms. Rebecca Winston, President, Winston Strategic Management Consultants

D

Workshop Agenda

SEPTEMBER 2, 2015

08:30	Welcome and Introductions
09:00	Discussion with Gen. Mark A. Welsh III, Chief of Staff, U.S. Air Force

Open Session 1—Communication Across Multiple Generations of Airmen

10:00	Lt. Gen. Steven Kwast, Commander, Air University
10:15	Brig. Gen. Kathleen Cook, Director of Public Affairs, Office of the Secretary of the Air Force
10:30	Discussion with Capt. Samuel "Ross" Hubbard, ACC/A5A10
11:00	Panel Discussion for Session 1
12:00	Working Lunch

Open Session 2—Comparing Communication Today Against Other Periods in History

13:00	Dr. Alan Vick, Senior Political Scientist, RAND Corporation
13:40	HON. F. Whitten Peters, Former Secretary of the Air Force
14:10	HON. James Roche, Former Secretary of the Air Force
14:40	Panel Discussion for Session 2
16:30	Day Wrap-Up Discussion
17:00	Adjourn for Day
18:00	Working Dinner

SEPTEMBER 3, 2015

08:30 Opening Remarks for Day 2

Open Session 3—Strategies for Effective Communication and Measures of Effectiveness

08:45 Dr. Brian Hoey, Principal, Hoey Group
09:30 Mr. Peter Debreceny, Senior Partner, Gagen-MacDonald
10:15 Mr. William Power, Fleishman-Hillard
11:00 Ms. Katie Paine, Founder and CEO, Paine Publishing, LLC
11:45 Panel Discussion for Session 3
12:30 Working Lunch

Open Session 4—Best Practices and Examples of Communication Strategies

13:30 Ms. Jennie Bledsoe, Director, Global Internal Communications, Goodyear Tire & Rubber Company
13:55 Maj. Gen. (U.S. Army, Ret.) Mari Eder, Former Head of Communications, U.S. Army; and President, Benson's Review, LLC
14:20 Dr. Vernon Miller, Associate Professor of Communication, Michigan State University
14:45 Mr. Ryan Henary, Managing Director, Internal Communications, FedEx Ground
15:10 Mr. Brian R. Ames, Vice President of Employee Communications, Boeing Company
15:35 Panel Discussion for Session 4
17:00 Day Wrap-Up Discussion
17:30 Adjourn for Day

SEPTEMBER 4, 2015

08:30 Opening Remarks for Day 3

Open Session 5—Role of Social Media in Effective Communication

08:45 Ms. Lois Kelly, Founder and CEO, Foghound
09:15 Mr. Robert Harles, Managing Director, Global Head of Social Media, Accenture Digital
09:45 Mr. Ed Terpening, Industrial Analyst, Altimeter Group
10:15 Mr. Ed Brill, Vice President of Social Business Cloud Services, IBM
10:45 Panel Discussion for Session 5
12:30 Working Lunch
13:30 Closed Session—Committee Only
16:00 Adjourn Workshop